Be sure to look for these titles in the *Go Parents!* series:

Teaching Your Children Good Manners
will help make teaching your children the
basics of good manners an entertaining and
(relatively) painless experience.

***Talking to Your Kids About Sex: From
Toddlers to Preteens*** takes a common-sense,
practical approach to helping parents talk to
children of a variety of ages and developmental levels about a topic that makes many
people uncomfortable.

Kid Disasters and How to Fix Them
takes on the common—and not so
common—household disasters kids can
cause, and provides hands-on, common
sense solutions that really work.

"Because I said So!" FAMILY Squabbles & how to handle them

a *Go Parents!* guide™

Nomad Press
A division of Nomad Communications
10 9 8 7 6 5 4 3 2 1
Copyright © 2003 Nomad Press

ISBN 0-9659258-5-4

Questions regarding the ordering of this book should be addressed to
Independent Publishers Group
814 N. Franklin St.
Chicago, IL 60610

Cover artwork and interior illustrations by Charles Woglom, Big Hed Designs
Design by Bruce Leasure
Edited by Susan Hale and Anna Typrowicz

Nomad Press, PO Box 875, Norwich, VT 05055
www.nomadpress.net

To Lisa and J, who taught me everything I know
about sibling rivalry

—LB

For Free

—SCA

1,202

Acknowledgments

Thanks to Steve Atkins, Charlie Woglom, Rachel Benoit, Susan Hale, Anna Typrowicz, Bruce Leasure, and everyone at Nomad Press for their suggestions, contributions and good humor during the production of this book. Thanks also to Richard, Sasha, Noah, and Simon, who can squabble with the best of them.

—LB

A heart felt "Thank You" to the families who have contributed to my clinical skills. These families continue to enhance my understanding of the "systemic dance" we all do.

I also want to recognize Staci, who I am proud to have as a sister and as one of my closest friends—despite the "family squabbles" we went through as kids. Let the record show that I freely acknowledge that most of our childhood squabbles may have been generated by me, her big brother. Staci is a model parent, teacher, and caring community member. We should all be so wealthy to have little sisters like mine.

—SCA

Table of Contents

"Because I Said So! That's Why!"

You open up the doors to your minivan and discover that the interior of your car is a rolling Superfund site. Backpacks, candy wrappers, old juice boxes, and random pieces of paper are strewn from end to end, so you go back inside and ask your kids to clean it out. Before you can finish saying, "Clean out the car" your kids start arguing.

"Why do I have to do it?" "I never leave a mess in the car." "The car's not that dirty—you can just step over that stuff, anyway." "It's too hot in the car! I'll get sick to my stomach." "I don't know how to clean it up. I'm too little."

No labor lawyer on earth could outlast your children in negotiations over why they shouldn't perform the task you ask them to accomplish. You are stuck either doing the job yourself because it takes less time than arguing with your little Johnnie Cochrans, or resorting to your favorite phrase, "Why do you have to do it? Because I said so!"

Sound familiar? Don't worry—help is at hand. ***"Because I Said So!" Family Squabbles and How to Handle Them*** takes on the most common areas of family friction—those altercations and annoying behaviors that drive parents nuts—and offers quick and practical advice for how to handle them.

Everyday squabbles, from hassles over homework to kids who break their curfew or tattle on one another are covered in detail, complete with solutions, helpful hints, and interesting bits of information that you never thought you'd need—until you became a parent.

How to Use This Book

This book should be used as a guide; the squabbles depicted here have actually happened and certainly will again. The solutions are based on solid advice and common sense, and acknowledge that while family squabbles may drive you nuts, they can make you laugh—eventually.

The book is divided loosely into sections that address family squabbles in similar areas. Wondering how to avoid resorting to threats to get your kids to behave? Look in Section 1: **I Am Going to Turn This Car Around!** for solutions to problems with bickering, tattling, and general family mayhem. Section 2: **Nag,**

Nag, Nag has advice and suggestions for helping your family work together to keep the household running smoothly, and Section 3: **Crime and Punishment** addresses those times when life, liberty and the pursuit of happiness run afoul of family law. Finally, the last section, **Ideas and Suggestions for Family Serenity** is an appendix that offers advice and helpful hints for maintaining your family's sanity, including a list of age-appropriate household chores and suggestions for family rules.

Surviving Family Squabbles

Whether you're facing off against your mutinous preteen, dealing with an adolescent on hormone overload, or trying to cope with your "No, no, no!"-torious toddler, keep in mind the following survival skills to get you through the trying times of being a parent.

Know when to say when. Sometimes the hardest thing for kids is to back away from a confrontational situation, so make it easier by stepping aside first.

Keep the lines of communication open. Your kids may be driving you nuts because they have stuff on their mind that they aren't ready to talk about—or don't even know is bothering them. Listen carefully to what they say to you, and let them finish griping or explaining before you jump in either to dismiss or try to solve their problem. Sometimes all they need is a willing and open ear.

Shake it off. It's hard not to stay mad when your kids have spent an entire afternoon arguing with each other, but it's important to shake off your resentment and move on when conflicts are over. Kids have an amazing ability to fight like tigers one minute and the next minute move happily on to another activity. Take your cue from them and move on to a better, happier place. Think of it as Mommy or Daddy Nirvana.

Model good behavior. If you want your kids to pitch in and help, treat each other with respect, and in general be good, productive citizens of your world, show them how. You are your kids' most important role model, so demonstrate through your own actions what you would like them to be.

Maintain a sense of humor. Sure, it's not funny right NOW that your kids are tattling like maniacs, or that your son wants you to pay him to clean his own room, but remember that the things that drive you nuts right now will make great family stories a couple of years down the road.

And remember that while every day as a parent is an opportunity to say, "Because I said so!," you can learn strategies for coping with family friction to help you enjoy, rather than endure, parenthood.

Section 1

I Am Going to Turn This Car Around!

Incidents of Bickering, Tattling, Surliness, and General Family Mayhem

Never Can Say Goodbye

You and your kids are at a neighborhood picnic, enjoying the happy bedlam that only cluster housing and potluck food can induce. Your kids are playing a giant game of kick ball, and you're happily being updated on every tidbit of neighborhood news. Life is good.

The festivities slowly wind down and you're ready to head back home. You track down your kids to give them the "time to go" signal. Two come trotting up, panting and sweaty. Your eight-year-old son, however, pretends not to notice you. You then call him, and he develops a sudden case of deafness. Finally, you head over to the kickball game to collect him in person, and your usually charming child is suddenly transformed into Damien from *The Omen*.

He starts to argue that it's too early to leave, the game isn't over, no one else is going home yet, and he doesn't think you're being fair. Being firm but friendly, you tell him you're glad he had a great time but it's time to go home. Now.

He slams the kickball on the ground, stomps his feet, and yells, "I don't want to go! You're being so mean!" Then he stomps off toward the car, waving his arms and muttering to himself about the injustice of being your son, while you trail behind, carrying a bowl of leftover potato salad and a potload of guilt.

What just happened, and how do you get your children to obey you without a big fuss?

The Solution

Most children find transition times difficult—especially abrupt ones. One of the great things about kids is their ability to completely immerse themselves in whatever activity they are participating in. Because they are so invested in the moment, it's hard for them to snap out of an activity and move on to something else, especially if they are enjoying what they are doing.

Plan ahead next time: call your son over a little before you're ready to leave and tell him in private what your plans are for leaving. This will allow you to have his undivided attention and will avoid a confrontation in front of his friends. Give him a specific amount of time as a countdown to your departure. This will give him some transition time and also allow him to maintain some control over his situation. Rather than having to be told to leave in front of his friends, he can tell his friends on his own.

Here's What to Do

- Give your kids some parameters before you arrive at a function or activity, so they have a rough idea of how long you'll stay and when you'll want to leave.

- Establish an agreed-upon routine for the exit plans. For example, let your kids know that you'll give them a ten-minute warning, a five-minute warning, a one-minute warning, and then the departure signal.

- Be sure to establish an agreed-upon punishment for not following the departure routine.

- At the end of the countdown make sure you actually leave— you need to respect your own rules if you expect your kids to respect them, too.

Helpful Hint

You may find that older kids don't need a countdown, and they'll probably resent you running up to them saying, "Honey, ten-minute warning." Instead, give them a general departure time, such as, "Keep in mind that we're leaving at eight-thirty." This method shows your older kids that you know they can keep track of their time on their own, and that you trust them to respect the limits you set. And if that doesn't work, you can always go back to the little-kid countdown.

Did Not, Did Too!

You're in the car on the way to a family outing. Your kids are happily settled in the back seat yakking away to each other, you're in a great mood, and the world is a beautiful place. You drive for awhile, absently listening to the radio and enjoying the scenery, when you hear from the backseat those words you hate: "Did not!" "Did too!"

Ah, your family mantra. Your kids are bickering again, and it's going to drive you completely nuts. Your destination suddenly seems much too far away.

How do you help your kids stop the constant rounds of petty arguments and get them to work out their problems alone—and preferably more quietly?

The Solution

Break out the ear plugs, turn up the radio, hum to yourself as loudly as possible, and stay out of it. Kids bicker because they can, and they do it when they are bored, tired, irritable, or just because it's their right as siblings. They want attention, and if negative attention is the way to get it, that's okay with them, too

One of the hardest things about being a parent is knowing when to step in and when to stand back when your kids are squabbling. If you always come to your children's rescue when they can't work out a problem, they will never learn to develop the social skills necessary to negotiate fair use of the Playstation, or learn how to share Barbies, or even brainstorm how to entertain themselves for fifteen minutes without you orchestrating their activities. Besides, no matter how diplomatic you try to be when you step in, you're bound to be perceived as playing favorites.

That said, it'll be easier for your kids to work out solutions on their own if they have the tools to do it—after all, it's not like screaming, "It's my turn, you butthead!" at the top of their lungs is an ideal solution from your kids' perspective, either. So play the role of initial arbitrator: help your kids set up some guidelines for working out their problems, and leave them to it. Otherwise, the only consequence of getting involved in your kids' petty arguments is that pretty soon they won't hate each other, they'll hate you instead.

Helpful Hint

If you and your partner are in the car together and your kids' bickering is getting to be more than you can stand, pull over and start kissing. It will stop any other activity in the car, guaranteed. Your kids will be so grossed out they'll promise virtually anything not to see it again.

Here's What to Do

- Give your kids some parameters for negotiating their own solution, including a time limit to resolve the issue and a consequence for each of them if they can't resolve the issue on their own.

- Make sure they know the rules about hitting or any other kid-on-kid violence, and the consequences for getting physical with each other—and make sure you enforce those consequences if your kids do come out swinging.

- Stand back and let them negotiate a mutually acceptable solution.

- If they are unable to come up with a solution within the allotted time period, enforce the consequence you have agreed upon.

- When they do work out the problem on their own, be sure to praise them. Positive reinforcement goes a very long way toward repeat good behavior.

Be aware that you're providing the tools for your kids to work out small squabbles, not big problems. You'll need to determine if the situation is too complicated or potentially dangerous for them to resolve themselves. If the conflict between your kids involves serious stuff like property damage or continued violence, then you will have to step in and take charge.

What's For Dinner?

Your family has been in a serious dinner rut lately, so you decide to break out of the vicious cycle of chicken nuggets, frozen pizza, and fish sticks and make your grandmother's famous homemade lasagna. You make a special trip to the store and get all the ingredients you'll need, you spend a couple of hours cooking up a storm, and the result is perfect. Your dinner looks like an ad for The Olive Garden and you're thinking that "Professional Chef" could be your new occupation.

You're contemplating starting your own cooking school when your son walks in and says, "What's for dinner?"

You proudly show him your fantastic lasagna and wait for the compliments. Instead, he says, "Oh, yuck—you know I hate lasagna. Do I have to have that for dinner? Can't you just make me a sandwich, instead?"

So here you are, stuck with your incredible creation and a picky eater, and you don't know what to do next: make him a sandwich or an ultimatum. Do you give in and make a special, custom-made dinner for the kid who won't eat what you're serving, or do you stand tough and say the menu is fixed and there are no substitutes? How do you get your kids to eat what you make for dinner and try new foods without whining about it?

Interesting info:

Eating together does more than promote good nutrition and a chance to see each other's faces more often: studies have shown that eating together increases family harmony and decreases the amount of acting out kids do. So sit down and eat up!

The Solution

The old adage, "You can't please all of the people all of the time," is never more true than about food. Sure, your kids would probably love it if you acted like their own personal short order cook, but learning to accept a less-than-perfect situation, whether it's coping with a dinner they don't like, or not getting their own way in another context, is a lesson that your kids need to learn about life. So don't make a special meal for your children simply because they don't want what you're cooking.

Instead, set the ground rules with your kids so that they know what your family policy is regarding meal times, and be sure to include them in the meal planning and preparation process so they have an opportunity to be a part of (and have a say in) what you make and eat.

You can help make every mealtime a win-win situation by trying to include at least one dish you know your kids will like. Not only will everyone have something he or she will eat and enjoy, but they also might be more open to trying something new. In addition, you'll get to spend a bit more time together—something that's becoming a pretty scarce commodity these days.

Here's What to Do

- Sit down with your kids and let them know your general family policy is "One family, one dinner menu," with a few key substitutes: if you know there are some dishes that various family members despise (or are allergic to), agree on one or two simple and healthy substitutes for those dishes that are also convenient for the cook that will keep everyone happy and well-fed.

- Let your kids be a part of the process: allow your kids to have some input in the week's menu, and let them choose and prepare complementary dishes that can be a part of every dinner.

- Every so often let your kids choose their favorite dinner, no matter how repugnant to you.

Helpful Hint

One way to get your kids to try new foods is to create "No thank you" helpings: a very small, bite-sized portion that they can eat in one bite. It's often easier for kids to experiment with food when they have a manageable portion on their plate. They can always ask for more, and they don't have to spend their entire meal trying to hide what they didn't eat.

Having The Last Words—
And Eating Them, Too

You and your kids are at the video store to pick out a couple of movies for the night. You know this can be a tricky business, so you set up some ground rules before you get started: your kids know what movie ratings are okay to choose, and each kid can pick out a movie, but you retain ultimate veto power if you think the movie is inappropriate for any reason—no matter what its rating. Your kids agree and off they go.

Your son chooses his movie in about five minutes. It's the latest installment in an endless series of animated adventures of a bunch of young dinosaurs. Having endured the last ten episodes, you personally can't wait for the episode that will wipe them all out with a giant asteroid and put an end to your cinematic misery, but it's acceptable fare and passes your inspection.

Your older daughter, on the other hand, is having more trouble with her decision. After picking up and putting down the same movie five times, she finally brings it over, ready to go. You read the back and realize that the content is more mature than she's ready to handle, so you explain why it's not right for your family, and you veto it.

Veto doesn't go over well with your daughter. She says, "But it's fine, really. All my friends have seen it."

Again, you veto it, and remind her of the rules you set and agreed to, and tell her to make another choice. She says, "But I really want this one. It's okay, really—there's nothing bad in it. Look at the rating!"

Veto. "But this is the only movie I found that I like!" She starts to pout.

Veto. "But there aren't any other movies here that are any good!" Pouting turns to sulking.

Veto. "But I don't want any other movie! I want this one!" Sulking turns to shouting.

At this point you pay for your son's choice, and leave the store with your daughter in a full blown tantrum behind you, still intent on getting you to change your mind, with every sentence beginning with, "But!"

How can you teach your kids that the last word isn't always the best word?

The Solution

The best way to teach your kids that "No" really does mean "No" is to set your house rules, let your kids know what they are, and stick to them—every time—regardless how much they whine, beg, plead, or have tantrums for you to bend them. Every family will have a different set of rules, and your children will inevitably think yours are too restrictive. But you've made your house rules based on your family's values, and it's important to have faith in yourself. You've made good choices and set appropriate limits for your family, so feel confident about enforcing them. Remember that being a parent is not an issue of being liked, but of being respected. Consistently enforcing reasonable rules will create that respect; enforcing them only when doing so doesn't make anyone unhappy, won't.

Here's What to Do

- Don't give in and let your daughter get the movie. Explain what specifically about the movie you don't like. By explaining your reasons for rejecting the movie, you'll demonstrate that your decision isn't just an arbitrary one designed to spoil her fun (although it's likely she'll think that, anyway).

- If possible, give your daughter a few minutes to cool down and go back in to the movie store when she's had a chance to collect herself and rethink her choices. You won't have compromised your family rules, and she will have the opportunity to choose another, more appropriate movie, so you both win.

- If your daughter can manage to pull herself together and make a better movie choice, remember to praise her for making a good decision—about the movie and about her reaction.

- If she's unable to move on and make a better choice after five minutes or so, end the trip. Let your daughter know that the window of opportunity has closed, and that you hope she'll make a better choice next time.

Sulking—The Gift That Keeps On Giving

Your daughter has decided to spend the day sulking around the house. You're not sure what initially set her off, but apparently nothing you or anyone else can say will make her happy. And if she's not happy, she's going to make sure no one else is, either. She oozes her way around the house, spreading her crabby mood around like a virus. When everyone else is sufficiently infected and sniping at each other, you lose your cool. You tell her to stay away from the rest of the family until she can be pleasant. She looks at you, hurt, and says, "Why are you always in such a bad mood?"

What now?

The Solution

Just because your kids are making you miserable doesn't mean they are happy about it—and in many cases, they really aren't aware of how their bad mood is affecting anyone else. Kids in general are very self-focused. Not only are they usually not intentionally going out of their way to make people around them crabby, they are often genuinely surprised and a little put out when they discover that they don't have exclusive rights on feeling out-of-sorts.

Regardless whether your kids are cluelessly ruining everyone's day or working hard to make sure you notice just how badly they're feeling, chances are that what they need is some positive attention—with some limits. You don't need to spend your entire afternoon wandering after your daughter asking over and over, "Honey, what's wrong?" but you can listen to what she has to say, empathize and validate her feelings, and try to help her find some positive aspect (however small) in her situation.

Here's What to Do

- Be an active observer. Comment on how you see her acting, but not in a judgmental way. For example, you could say, "I notice you're upset no matter what your dad says."

- Validate your child's point of view—don't ignore it altogether or try to change the subject or brush it off. Legitimize her feelings. For example, you could say, "It seems that a lot of things that don't normally bother you are really getting to you today. It sounds like you're frustrated."

- Rephrase the negative into a positive and connect it to your child's life in some way without trivializing the problem. Kids are more likely to be receptive to a positive viewpoint if it's related to helping solve a specific problem. For example, rather than saying, "I know you're disappointed that you didn't get the role you wanted in the play, but cheer up—there will be other plays," you could say, "I know it wasn't your first choice, but the part you were cast in is also a real challenge. I know you're up to it."

- Remember that listening to your kids' gripes and validating what they have to say will not only allow them to air some of their grievances, it will also help them become more aware of what they're feeling. It may even give them a clue about how their behavior affects other family members' moods, too.

Helpful Hint

Never underestimate the power of a good distraction to help you and your kids bounce back from a bad mood. Play a board game, go for a walk, head out for a bite to eat, see what's at the movies: sometimes just getting out of the house can disperse the bad karma. Also, remember that it's important not to take anything your kids say too personally since inevitably whatever the problem your child is experiencing will be portrayed as your fault.

Calgon, Take Me Away!

You're in the very crowded grocery store and you're at the end of your list—and your patience. Your very crabby preschooler is whining at you, perched on top of a precarious pile of frozen food, something is dripping from the bottom of the cart, and your other kids are dragging behind, occasionally trying to sneak bags of artificially-flavored everything into the cart while you're not looking.

In the packed checkout line, your pre-schooler sees a small toy hanging from a rack. He says, "Can I get this?" You make the critical mistake of picking it up for a closer inspection. No surprise, it's a piece of junk—so you put it back and say no.

Wrong answer.

Your preschooler blows like a pint-sized Vesuvius, kicking and screaming, "I want it, I want it!" His decibel level is remarkable. Half of your groceries are in the cart, the other half soggily moving down the belt to the bagging area, so leaving the store isn't an option. Your other kids skulk over to the gumball machines and pretend they aren't with you, while everyone else in the store is staring to see what is causing the horrible commotion.

So—do you give in just this once and give your preschooler the toy to shut him up, or do you pretend he's not perforating your eardrums and making you feel like the world's worst parent, tough it out, and finish your shopping?

The Solution

Ah, these are the times that try parents' souls. But regardless how long or loud your preschooler yells, it's never a good idea to reward behavior you don't want repeated. You may think you have bought yourself a cheapo toy and a few minutes' peace, but your preschooler will remember that his screaming resulted in getting what he wanted—and you can be sure he'll use the same method again.

Here's What to Do

- Do NOT give your child the toy: you'd only be reinforcing the idea that screaming like a siren will get him what he wants. Also, don't offer him an alternative item as a distraction. A peace offering will give him the same message as the toy—that screaming works.

- Don't freak out at your child, regardless how much you may want to. He'll feed off your stress and get worse.

- Stay as calm as you can, and try to keep your child from hurting himself. Attempt to help your child find the words to describe what he's going through—you can say things like, "You seem very upset. You really wanted that toy, didn't you?' Validate his feelings about wanting something and empathize with him. It may help him calm down.

- Do NOT worry about what other people are thinking about you. You'll never win this one: half will be annoyed and think you're a bad parent because you won't give him the darn toy so he'll stop screaming and the other half will be annoyed and think you're a bad parent because he's screaming and you're not punishing him for it.

- Keep loading those groceries onto the belt as fast as you possibly can.

Helpful Hint

From a preschooler's perspective, grocery shopping is totally unfair: he has to sit in the cart and watch while you get to do everything fun. Let your child become part of the process so he'll be more vested in a successful trip from start to finish. Let him make a few choices, such as what kind of cookies or Popsicles to buy, and let him help unload some of the (unbreakable) groceries at the checkout. The more you can keep your little guys busy and part of the process, the less likely you are to have meltdowns at inopportune times.

Tell It to The Judge

It's one week into summer vacation and your children are spending the day playing their favorite game, "I'm Telling." They parade up to you, one after another, all day long, ratting on each other with ferocious glee. "Mom, he said a word that we're not supposed to say. Wanna hear it?" "Mom, she touched my leg and I said, 'Don't do that,' and then I hit her by accident." "But she called me a moron first!" "I took it because I told him to share and he wouldn't." You feel like the star in a home–movie version of Judge Judy. How do you get your kids to solve their own problems without constantly dragging you in the middle?

The Solution

As much as your children would love your attention and involvement 24-7, they need to learn how to make their own fun and solve their own problems. If you have to step in to resolve every conflict they have, or come up with entertainment every time they are bored, they will never learn to work things out or occupy themselves independently. With that said, the ages of your children will obviously dictate how much tattling and parental intervention is necessary. If you're dealing with a pack of two-year olds, you're going to have to do a lot more hands-on parenting and refereeing than if your kids are older and developmentally capable of coming up with solutions to their disagreements on their own.

Every family should have some basic ground rules for what is and isn't acceptable behavior, as well as clear consequences for breaking those rules. Make a list of house rules that are age appropriate for your family members and go over them with all of your children. Keep the list posted somewhere so that everyone in the house—kids and guests included—can refer to them.

Here's What to Do

- Help your kids learn to do a quick check before coming to report to you by asking themselves the following questions:

  - Is anyone hurt?
  - Are house rules being broken?
  - Am I prepared for the consequences?
  - Do I know what those consequences are?
  - Do I still want to tell?

- Let your older kids know that forewarned is forearmed: you want to hear about it if someone is hurt or if a house rule is broken; otherwise, they need to try to resolve their problems themselves. A good way to help your kids avoid tattling, just because they can, is to have the consequences for breaking house rules apply to false reports, too.

- You'll still probably say, "Work it out," a million times or more during your lifetime, but gradually your kids will rely on you less to solve their problems if they are prepared to negotiate their own disputes.

Helpful Hint

Absence really does make the heart grow fonder. If your kids are mixing like oil and water, you can try the "three strikes" rule. Let them know that if you have to intervene three times, they will each be assigned a job as a forfeit, and explain the jobs that face them if they can't work out their disputes independently. This helps turn conflict resolution into a game, and also raises the stakes for getting along more peacefully. Playing together will look much more appealing from behind a broom or while folding laundry.

What a Bummer

Your son's class has planned a whale watching field trip since the first day of school. The class spent the entire school year learning about the mighty mammal, and your son has become a walking encyclopedia about whales, from what they eat to how they give birth—and he shares all the details at every opportunity. You're looking forward to the whale watch almost as much as he is, if for no other reason than to be able to talk about something else at the dinner table.

At last the day of the whale watch dawns—dark and rainy. You drive a car full of incredibly excited children all the way to the beach, only to discover that the ocean looks like the set of *The Perfect Storm*, and the whale watch company has decided to cancel the trip because of the weather.

Everyone is disappointed, but no one more so than your son. In fact, even when the other kids perk up at an alternative plan, he continues to sulk and whine, and seems hell bent on ruining what's left of the trip. How do you help your kids learn how to cope with disappointment and move on while the moving's good?

The Solution

It's hard for anyone not to be disappointed whenever there is a big change in plans, especially if there has been considerable build up to the cancelled event. And usually the reaction kids have to disappointment reflects their personalities: kids who are flexible tend to get over abrupt changes in plans pretty quickly and go with the flow, while kids who like to know exactly what's coming next and tend to be very invested in a planned activity can be absolutely devastated if those plans change.

The best way to help kids who have a hard time moving on when plans change unexpectedly is to immediately resolve the ambiguity over whether or not they'll ever get to do the activity that's been cancelled. Better yet, set a definite new date for the activity so that they can reset their expectations for the missed activity and then start to focus on the one that has just been presented to them.

It can be hard for parents to be patient with their kids if they see all the other kids shaking off their disappointment and becoming involved in an alternative activity, but it's important not to shame your kids if they are having a hard time letting go of those feelings, especially not in front of their friends. Let your child know that it is disappointing when plans get changed, and it's okay to feel that way, then ask your child to come up with some ideas for how to handle this feeling. You may find that redirecting his energy into coming up with solutions to the way he is feeling helps make him feel more in control of his situation and thus more positive about its outcome.

Here's What to Do

- Take your son off to the side or to a more private location.

- Let him vent his feelings for a bit in a safe and private place; empathize with him about feeling disappointed.

- Ask your son to come up with some ways to handle how he's feeling.

- Make sure your son knows the event will be rescheduled, and if possible, set a date immediately for the make-up.

Helpful Hint

For some kids, it's not necessarily the particular event that matters so much, but rather the sense of knowing what is coming and feeling in control of their environment that makes it so difficult to accept disappointment when plans change. You might consider tempering expectations with some caveats such as, "if the weather is okay," or "we'll have to see what happens," so that you aren't promising absolutes if you can't absolutely guarantee them.

Helping Your Kid Out of a Jam

Your teenager is invited to an acquaintance's house for a party. Her best friends are allowed to go, so she's been surprisingly willing to adhere to your family rules: she found out if parents will be there, retrieved the phone number, and even stood beside you while you made the call to confirm that her friend's Mom and Dad would be in attendance at the gala event.

The night of the party arrives and you send off your perfumed daughter to meet her friends with your blessing and a cell phone. A couple of hours after she leaves your phone rings. On the other end is your daughter, speaking into the phone like a secret agent. You can barely hear her over the din surrounding her.

"We went to the party but it was totally boring, so we left to go to the movies. But we ran into some friends who heard about another party, and we went with them," she whispers. "Now we're here, but it's totally out of control, I don't know anyone, and I don't want to stay—but I don't want to look like a jerk in front of my friends."

You're torn between being proud of your daughter for calling you, and furious that she'd put herself in such a stupid situation. But you realize that you need to address one problem at a time, and this is a no-brainer—you tell her to walk into the room where her friends are, holding the phone to her ear and say, "Okay, I'll be right home." But what about next time? How can you help make sure that your daughter always has a way out of a sticky situation?

The Solution

The best way to ensure that your kids have a way out of uncomfortable situations is to follow the Scouting motto: always be prepared.

First, make it a family rule that your kids have to call to let you know any and every time there is a change in their plans. Then sit down with your kids and make an "escape pact" that they can follow when they feel the need to make a face-saving exit.

A family escape pact will involve, first and foremost, trust on both your parts. The first—and potentially most difficult for you—step will be to agree mutually that no matter what the circumstances are for your kids needing an exit, calling you for help is safe. That means that the questions you have about why your kids are at a party at someone's house they don't even know, or why their breath smells like peppermint schnapps, need to wait until they are home, safe and sound, and able to talk rationally about their experience. If your kids are uncomfortable enough about the situation they are in to activate their escape plan, it's important to reinforce positively the good decision they made by calling you. Explanations and recriminations can wait.

Here's What to Do

- Before they go out for an evening or take off with their friends, make sure your kids have a way of contacting you if they need to.

- Come up with a code word or phrase that they can use to let you know they want to leave the situation they are in without having to admit it in front of their friends. For example, "armadillo" weaved into the conversation means, "Come get me right now!"

- If they don't have a cell phone, make sure they have a calling card and know how to use it.

- Reiterate your rule about calling to tell you if their plans change.

- Always be willing to be the excuse your kids can use for making an exit: make it a policy that your kids have to call at a certain time to check in, and if they need to, they can say, "If I don't call home at 10:00, my too-involved, smothering parents will ground me for next weekend." This is a great all-purpose excuse that takes the responsibility off your kids' shoulders.

Helpful Hint

Struggling to think up a great code phrase your kids could use for their family escape pact? Here are a few tried-and-true phrases your kids can say when they are in a jam and want to leave without actually saying so:
- *"I'm really tired."*
- *"I'm not feeling very well."*
- *"I promised I'd call."*
- *"I forgot we have to get up early tomorrow."*
- *"What? You need me home now?"*

Section 2
Nag, Nag, Nag!

*Chores, Responsibilities, Money,
and Other Annoyances*

Chaos—It's What's For Breakfast

It's 8 A.M. Your kids have just left for school, you haven't even begun to get ready for work, and you feel like you've already put in a full day at the salt mines. You survey the damage: your kitchen looks like a cereal bomb went off in it, although you're not certain anyone actually ate any breakfast. Clothes, shoes, papers, and breakfast dishes are scattered everywhere, and you're pretty sure your son got out of the house wearing the same shirt he's had on for at least two days. The permission slip that your daughter had a fit about you signing to turn in today is lying on the table, right where she left it, and you notice that someone forgot his lunch. Just another typical morning at your house.

No matter how early you get started, when it's time to go to school no one is quite ready, and you're left yelling, "Let's go!

Let's go!" like some demented cowpoke herding your steers to market. How can you help your kids make the transition from home to school without feeling like you're on a TV Land episode of *Bonanza*?

The Solution

There's nothing that says lovin' like a snarling mother booting her kids out the door in the morning. Kids need to learn to be responsible for their own possessions, schedules, lunches, backpacks, homework, and sports equipment—but they aren't likely to learn to be organized in the hour or so between the time they wake up in the morning and the time they leave for school, especially if they are still in elementary or middle school.

So help your kids tone down their morning frenzy by giving them the tools to get themselves organized the night before—and check to make sure they've done it. Since the goal is for your kids—not you—to get themselves and their gear ready for school each morning, cut back and eventually stop checking to confirm that they have all of their stuff each night.

Here's What to Do

- Together with your kids make a list of the things each child needs to get ready, such as clean clothes, retainer, spelling words, or musical instrument.

- Designate an area for your kids to put their stuff each night. If they use backpacks, make sure the backpacks go to the same place every night so the kids aren't rushing to find them in the morning.

- Have your kids be responsible for collecting all their stuff. For kids in early elementary school, review their checklist for a week or so to make sure they are actually accomplishing the job. For children in kindergarten, give them only one responsibility to remember, such as placing their school folder or backpack in a designated spot the night before.

- After a week of checking your kids' list, stop and let them be responsible for getting their act together on their own. But you will have to remind them to get everything ready, even if you aren't checking each item.

- If your kids start forgetting things again, or your mornings are more hectic than usual, go back to the checklist.

Helpful Hint

It's unlikely that your older middle school or high-school age kids are going to want to sit down and make a "What I Need For School" list with you OR will want you to check their backpacks the night before to make sure everything is in there. And that's fine—but you should make it clear to your older kids that they are responsible for their own belongings, and you won't be bailing them out if they forget that important history report or their own lunch when it's Lunchlady Special day at the cafeteria. And if they keep forgetting their stuff or being incredibly disorganized, it's time to have a candid parent-child conversation about how you can help them become organized until they are successful. Forewarned is forearmed.

Fetch Me My Slippers

You're racing from one end of your house to the other, tidying here, cleaning there. Your kids, meanwhile, are draped over the furniture in the family room, practically comatose, watching TV. Your son has an empty water glass in front of him. As you rush by like a cleaning whirling dervish, he glances up and say, "Hey, mom—as long as you're up, could you refill my water? Oh, and your head is blocking the screen."

Suddenly it dawns on you—somewhere along the line you've been demoted from head of household to simply head of house-keeping. How do you get your kids to view you as more than their personal indentured servant?

The Solution

As smart and wonderful as your children are, they aren't mind readers, and kids by nature are focused on one thing—themselves. Unless it directly affects them, kids

tend to look at the big picture, rather than the little one—they see the big-screen TV and the comfy couch, not the pile of laundry that needs to be folded on top of it. So what do they do? They push the laundry out of the way and make themselves at home.

The best way to get your kids regularly doing jobs and helping around the house is to establish a predictable routine for jobs and job assignments, and let the kids be part of the planning process. There are certain jobs that no one wants to do, but there are others that some kids enjoy more than others—use that to your advantage. Assign chores that must be done on a regular basis and on a specific time schedule.

Here's What to Do

- Assign your kids specific jobs, taking into account age, ability, and special circumstances. (If your kids regularly get home from school at 7 P.M. because of sports, school activities, or other jobs, for example, a weekday job that they can't possibly manage is going to lead to disaster.) Be realistic.

- Let your kids be part of the job-assignment process.

- Establish a schedule of deadlines for the jobs and the consequences and/or rewards for accomplishing them. (For example, their beds must be made and rooms tidied before they leave for school; if they can't manage that, they'll have to get up earlier.)

- Make it clear that jobs have to be done before leisure time begins.

It'll take quite a bit of supervision at first, but the more you reinforce the schedule of chore followed by reward, your kids will adapt to the new routine—and you'll feel less like your family's maid.

Helpful Hint

The more specific you can be about what you want the outcome of their chore to be, the happier both you and they will be. If you simply say, "Clean up your room," your kid will look at his room and answer, "It is," even if it looks like a tornado came through it. Instead, say, "Make your bed, put all the clothes in the drawers, pick up and organize all the books and papers on the floor, and vacuum the rug."

Helpful Hint

If you have a big family job, such as raking the yard, cleaning out the garage, or spring cleaning the attic, and you want your kids to be happy members of the team (or at least not whining members of the team), plan for success:

- *Break the job down into manageable junks. For example, if you're raking the yard, divide it into four quadrants and tackle each one individually. Schedule breaks so that your kids don't view the job as a day at the gulag.*
- *Make it fun: Turn the job into a contest. For example, while you're raking, have a contest to see how fast you all can rake up each area, setting new time goals for each one. If you beat your projected time, you could award your kids some kind of small reward.*
- *Make it worthwhile: Tell your kids beforehand that if you can finish the family job, you can all have a family treat, such as going out to dinner, or to a movie.*

"E" Doesn't Mean
"Excellent Trip!"

Your daughter recently passed her driver's test and is the proud owner of a new license. She loves the freedom driving a car provides, and you love that she can occasionally drive her younger siblings to school. She takes to life on the open road with the dedication of a long-distance trucker, and you all bask in the glow of exhaust fumes and family cooperation.

Until a month or so later, when you realize that every time you get in the car after your daughter has been driving, the gas gauge is on Empty. It dawns on you that while your daughter excels at driving the car, she apparently doesn't like paying for its upkeep.

When you bring up the fact that the car runs on fuel that can be purchased at gas stations virtually anywhere in town, she bristles and says, "But I'm helping you when I drive the car! Why should I have to pay for that?"

You don't want to lose your taxi service, but Little Miss Earnhardt spends a lot more time driving her friends around than her family, and your gas budget has gone out the window.

What now?

The Solution

Driving the family car is a privilege, not a birthright, regardless what most sixteen-year olds believe. Being treated like an adult and given the use of the car carries with it the responsibility of being considerate of the other drivers in the family. If your daughter is old enough to drive a car and responsible enough to be trusted with a family possession, she should also be responsible for helping with its upkeep. This should include keeping the car clean, avoiding parking it in areas where it might be vandalized or dented, and returning it on time and in good condition. In exchange, because your daughter does help you with errands and shuttle service, you can also be considerate of her needs: give her a gas allowance that will cover the trips you need her to make and a little extra, and make her use of the car contingent on it coming back to you with plenty of gas in the tank. Let her know that this is a non-negotiable rule: if she leaves the car on empty, she loses the privilege of using the car for a specific amount of time.

Here's What to Do

- Make an agreement with your daughter that the car has to come back to you with at least the same amount of gas it had when she left. The car should also come back clean and be available whenever you need it—which means keeping the keys in a mutually convenient location.

- Give her a monthly gas allowance that will cover the cost of any errand you may need her to run with a little more for good measure—this gives you leeway from month to month depending on the errand or carpool load.

- Allow her to budget her gas allowance on her own, keeping in mind the first rule: if she runs out of gas money, she's hoofing it.

Helpful Hint

Most gas stations now sell pre-paid gas cards, similar to calling cards. You can always buy one of these for your daughter so that you can be assured that the gas allowance you give her is going directly into the tank.

Music Lessons From Hell

Your daughter recently informed you that she's going to become a rock star, get rich and famous, and use her fame and fortune to take care of you in your old age. The only thing standing in her way is that she doesn't know how to play the guitar. She wheedles and begs, and you finally buy her the guitar, the music, the music stand, and lessons from the coolest teacher in town.

After two weeks of lessons and a case of sore fingertips, your daughter decides it's way too hard to play the guitar and she'd rather be a famous artist instead. Getting her to practice becomes punishment for both of you—and now you're left with a lot of musical equipment and a six-month commitment to the guitar teacher that is non-refundable. What do you do now?

The Solution

Think about how many times you've started a huge project and quit, simply because it seemed too overwhelming— that's probably what's happening here. Most kids need short, attainable goals to keep them interested in the big picture, and they need some immediate success to keep them positive about learning new skills.

The best chance for success with any large undertaking is to break down big projects into small, manageable blocks with a definite beginning and ending. For music lessons, agree with your child to commit to five lessons—and accompanying practice sessions—at a time. When the five lessons are up, re-assess how it is going.

Practicing a new skill is often the most difficult part of mastering it. If your kids are under 12 or so, it's unlikely that they'll be able to sustain motivation and the discipline to practice on their own. Plan to participate in practices at first, as a cheerleader. Your kids will love the time they get to spend with you. Also, most kids work best in short spurts. If your child is supposed to practice a half hour a day, break it down into ten-minute sessions.

Here's What to Do

- Before you make a huge investment, create a short-term "contract" that outlines the parameters of the commitment. Remember that the younger the child, the shorter the commitment should be.

- Rent, rather than buy, the musical instrument at first.

- Take part in practice sessions.

- Make sure the practice sessions are a reasonable amount of time, based on the age and your knowledge of your child.

- Re-assess how things are going at the end of the "contract" and go through the above steps again, slowly cutting back your own participation.

Helpful Hint

It's a good idea to try to match the instrument to the child—if you have a kid who doesn't have much patience or has trouble concentrating on the best of days, starting off with an instrument that offers immediate success, such as a piano or recorder, might be a good idea.

Be aware that many instrumental programs prefer to start students when they are in the fourth grade, since kids this age are usually better able to concentrate and remember what they are learning.

Also, taking lessons with your child is a great way to incorporate some one-on-one time with your child, encourage her to work on her skills, and learn some new ones of your own.

To Pay or Not to Pay

Your son wants a new bike, and you decide that this is the perfect opportunity to teach him the value of working toward a goal. You agree to pay half if he can come up with the rest.

He diligently heads out to earn the money—by working for other people. He rakes neighbors' leaves, cleans out garages, and destroys your kitchen while creating a one-man bake sale. Meanwhile, your own leaves pile up, your garage is full-to-bursting, and his bedroom—well, you don't even want to think about his room.

When you point this out to your son, he says, "I need to earn money. If you want me to help around here, you'll have to pay me like everyone else." This isn't quite what you had in mind when this whole project got started. You've created a monster with a dirty room and a yen for yen. What do you do now?

The Solution

Being part of a family carries with it a certain amount of responsibility—including basic chores that keep the family running smoothly. Every family member should have certain tasks for which they are responsible that aren't on a fee-for-service basis. Depending on the ages of your kids, this can range from feeding the dog to sorting the recycling or bringing out the garbage. Jobs that are above and beyond the basic call of duty can and should be available on an a la carte cash basis, but only after the basic chores are done.

Here's What to Do

- Make a list of the basic chores for which each child in your family is responsible. These are unpaid, non-negotiable chores.

- Post the chores on the fridge or someplace where everyone— kids and parents included—can refer to them any time. Make it clear that these chores need to be completed to an acceptable standard before any paying jobs get started. If you have family members for whom earning money isn't an enticement, make it clear that chores come before any other, fun activities—or that those family members will have to work to pay for the activities or extras they want, like movie tickets or candy.

- Create a list of paying chores that are available at your house. Offer the going rate, or at least close to it. Check to find out what the neighbors are paying, for example.

- Let your kids know that you have right of first refusal. That means that your garage gets cleaned out before your neighbor's.

- Offer a "mystery job" that pays a set amount of money (make it an enticing sum) that your kids can choose, sight unseen. Vary the mystery job from day to day or week to week, depending on when you assign your chores. Some weeks make the job challenging (such as washing windows), other weeks make it easy (such as watering the plants). It will keep your kids guessing, and most kids can't resist a surprise, regardless the outcome.

Helpful Hint

Want to figure out how many chores you should give your kid? Have one daily chore for every two years of your child's age (i.e., if he's ten, he should have five basic chores, such as making his bed, tidying his room, putting his dirty clothes in the laundry pile, helping set or clear the table, and taking out the trash). Remember to keep the chores age appropriate; after all, you don't want your five-year-old handling Granny's fancy china unless you're prepared for some serious breakage, and you also don't want the jobs to be so overwhelming that none of them gets accomplished.

The Brotherhood of The Traveling Pants

Your son needed new pants, so you went out for what you thought would be a quick trip for a pair of jeans. Four stores and eighty pairs of jeans later you learn that your son cares more about fit and look than you ever imagined. It turns out that the only socially acceptable, fully functioning, non-chafing pants he can wear cost way more than you were planning to spend. Your son promises he'll take good, good care of them, and you can't face another store, so The Pants come home with you. Your son wears them every day for a week, and suddenly they disappear. A couple of days go by, and you finally ask him where The Pants have gone. He looks at you blankly and says, "What pants?" You remind him about the eighty pairs of rejected jeans, The Pants, and his vow that he'll never let them leave his sight. He shrugs and says over his shoulder, "Oh, yeah—those. They ripped and I lost them at soccer practice. Hey, we're going to have to go shopping again, because now I don't have any pants to wear." The screen door slams and he disappears outside.

You're left with a hefty credit card bill, an invisible pair of the formerly coolest pair of pants in town, and a headache. How do you teach your kids to be responsible for the things you buy them?

The Solution

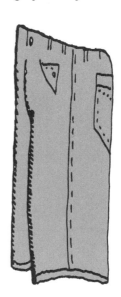

The best way to help kids learn to be responsible about the things you buy them is to invest them in the process— literally. When you are shopping for clothes for your child, assign a certain amount of money as a clothing budget, and let your kids be involved in the purchasing decisions—but also make it their responsibility to budget their wardrobe dollars. That means when the money is gone, it's gone, regardless what happens to the items they buy.

If your kids lose the clothes they buy with their clothing budget, they'll have to wear the clothes they have left. You should also offer them an opportunity to earn back the money it will take to buy new clothes. A good way to make this successful is to offer to come up with half of the cost of the item if they can earn the other half.

Remember that the goal of this is to teach your kids to be responsible for keeping track and taking care of their belongings with positive outcomes, so if something happens that's way beyond their control (stolen from their locked locker, for example, or ripped because they fell down the stairs), you'll need to take into account mitigating circumstances.

Here's What to Do

- Establish the amount of money you want your child to spend.

- Set the ground rules for what can and can't be bought—and the responsibilities involved (i.e., replacement policy).

- Take your kids shopping with calculator in hand (do it one child at a time).

- Let your child make purchasing decisions with your input.

Helpful Hint

Giving your kids a clothing budget is also a great way for them to begin to understand the value of a dollar, and the benefits of saving and investing their money. Some parents might consider encouraging their kids to leave a small reserve in their clothing "account" and over time pay "interest" on the principal for future purchases.

I'll Do It Later—Really!

It's 10:30 P.M. and your son hasn't done his homework. You asked him about it when he came home from school and he said, "I'll do it later." You asked him again at 4 P.M., when he came in from playing soccer. He said, "I'll do it later." You asked him again at 7:30, after you'd eaten dinner and he was online. He said, "I'll do it later." You asked him again at 8:30, when you settled down to watch a show and he joined you on the couch. He said, "I'll do it later."

At 10:30 you turn off the TV and tell your son it's bedtime. He says, "But I have to do my homework!"

What now?

The Solution

Most kids work harder on procrastinating than they ever do on their homework. After all, who wants to practice spelling words, do algebra problems, take out the trash, or do anything unpleasant when there's TV to watch, games to play, and general fooling around to do?

Kids need to learn to budget their time and be responsible for setting priorities, but they need help learning how to do it, especially if your kids are still in elementary or middle school. The best way to go about it is to help your kids create a consistent homework routine, where they go to the same, quiet place every day at the same time (or as close to it as possible) to do their school work.

They may complain about it, but kids thrive on routines, and having a consistent schedule and place for homework will help make completing it easier.

Here's What to Do

- Sit down with your kids and create a master calendar of activities, from sports practices to orthodontist appointments to school conferences, and block out a homework schedule.

- Involve your kids in the process so they have a sense of control and ownership over their schedule.

- Post the schedule where everyone can see it on a daily basis.

- Help your kids choose a space for them to do their homework. Avoid high traffic areas, or places where they are bound to get distracted.

- Remind your kids about their homework schedule, but don't badger them—they need to learn that completing their work is their responsibility, not yours.

- Make leisure time activities contingent on completing their homework: for example, no screen time until their homework is done, or no screen time during the school week, period.

Helpful Hint

So after all that, what happens if your kids don't follow through and do their homework? Let them know that while you'll help set the stage for good homework habits, actually doing the work is up to them. Be sure to discuss with your kids the consequences of not completing it, and make sure your kids know that if they don't get the work done, you won't be bailing them out with their teachers at school. For most kids, one detention or rescinded recess is enough to keep their motivation high.

Pump Up The Volume

It's dinner time and your whole family is at the table, eating together—just like in a Norman Rockwell painting. Your kids are using their utensils properly, their napkins are on their laps, and you kind of wish a neighbor or somebody would walk in so they could see what a nice family you are.

Until you make a tactical error and ask a general question: "So, what did you all do today?" Every member of your family tells you what he or she did, all at the same time, all at top volume. You patiently say, "Indoor voices," and "let's take turns," but apparently no one can hear you. You finally bang on the table with your fist and say, "Quiet!!" which gets their attention, but makes you feel a little like Nikita Kruschev—not really the persona you were going for.

Your kids know how to take turns and speak in tones that won't deafen the rest of the family, and you've seen them in action—especially at other people's houses. But somehow bedlam breaks out at your own dinner table more often than not. How do you keep the "family" in family dinners without going deaf or crazy?

The Solution

Good table manners take practice, and it's not simply a matter of learning which fork to use or saying please and thank you. Part of learning good table manners is learning to take turns being the center of attention. Family discussions, often even among adults, need moderators to help direct the conversation, determine if someone has had the floor too long, and help facilitate discussion and questions without bedlam breaking out. Since you're the adult here, you'll need to take on that role. Be the moderator at your table: assign one person at a time to talk about their day, and regulate how long that person can have the floor.

Here's What to Do

- At the start of dinner, assign yourself the role of moderator: choose one child and ask him or her a very specific question, such as to tell you one interesting thing that happened to them that day.

- Tell everyone else at the table that no one may speak until the first child is finished.

- After that child has told you one thing (and keep it to one thing, not one that leads to three others), let her choose the next person to tell. This helps your kids be part of the decision making process, and reinforces the idea that everyone will have a turn to talk.

- Set some ground rules for what one thing your kids can discuss. For example, your kids might want to talk about the one amazing dream they had—the telling of which could go on for hours. Keep the questions pointed and the discussion moving from one child to the next.

- After you've been the moderator of the family discussion for a week or so, authorizing your kids to take turns talking, give them a chance to take charge of the conversation on their own and see if they can moderate themselves. If the noise level gets too high or someone dominates the discussion too long, you can step in.

Helpful Hint

The more you can turn teaching table manners into a game, the more readily your kids will learn them. Try "I Spy Good Manners," a game where you award points each time you see your kids using good manners. The child with the highest number of points gets out of clearing his or her plate from the table.

Another game that reinforces good manners, is quiet, and also helps kids notice and comment on nice things about others is "The Compliment Game." Each person at the table gets a turn to give another person at the table a compliment. The person who is given the compliment says, "thank you," and compliments another person.

Hey, Restock My Wallet, Would You?

You decide that your kids are old enough to have certain chores that are above and beyond basic maintenance, and deserve to be part of a job-for-pay scenario. You have a family meeting and negotiate a weekly allowance for a certain number of chores done to a certain level of satisfaction.

For two weeks your house has never looked better, and your family is working together like a well-oiled machine. You feel better and better about this allowance thing, especially since your kids have never been more responsible or willing to pitch in to help. "After all," your son says, "we're getting paid for it."

And then a couple more weeks pass, and gradually the machine starts to break down. You're nagging more, they're helping less, and you find yourself saddled with more and more of the stuff you thought you had assigned to other family members.

The only constant is that each week your kids show up for payday with their wallets ready and waiting. Finally, you've had it. On payday you withhold the cash. Your kids look at you with shock and amazement. "But you owe us our allowance! You promised you'd pay us money each week!"

This is not a union house. You remember the good old days, when allowance was a new thing and everyone worked to get it. How do you get back to the golden age of honest pay for honest work at your house?

The Solution

Kids usually don't get the idea of doing a job well for its intrinsic value. If the job is to put the clothes away in their drawers, what does it matter if they aren't folded first? The result is the same, and it takes less time. Generally speaking, kids want to get the work over with and get back to what they were doing. If they can get away with doing a crummy job and still get paid for it, all the better. So take charge and do what real employers do: negotiate a contract and conduct job reviews. Be specific about the quality of the work you expect and when it needs to be completed, and set specific inspection dates and times. If the job is lousy, don't pay them; if it's over and above what you've negotiated, give them a raise. Money talks—and when it walks, your kids will notice.

Here's What to Do:

- Create a contract with each child that includes a checklist for exactly what each job entails. For example, if you hire them to clean out your car each week, the checklist might read:

  1. Clean out all trash, clothes, toys, and books.
  2. Vacuum all floors and seats.
  3. Clean all windows.

- Specify a date and time that the jobs need to be finished.

- Make sure your children and you both sign the contract.

- Inspect the jobs on schedule, and assess how well the job is done.

If the quality of the job isn't up to standard, be sure to be specific about what needs to be changed or re-done to make it acceptable, and then give your child the opportunity to make it right and still get paid.

Helpful Hint

If you have younger kids and you're having trouble getting them to focus on chores, turn it into a contest: offer to time them to see how much they can accomplish by the time you count to ten (or in a minute, or whatever time you choose). Be sure to keep the time limit fairly short so they can maintain both interest and enthusiasm, but it's amazing how motivated little kids are by the idea of working under pressure.

Section 3
Crime and Punishment

*When Life, Liberty, and the Pursuit of Happiness
Run Afoul of Family Law*

Book 'Em, Danno

Your son is invited to spend the night at his friend's house. A few hours before the sleepover, his friend calls and asks if your son can go with him to the movies—they have a choice between a comedy and the newest scary movie, *Shriek 3*. You checked the rating and the reviews, and decide it's just not a movie you want him to see. You've known your son for a long time, and don't look forward to spending every night for the next month with half the upstairs lights on and a "monster check" update every fifteen minutes. So you tell him that he's allowed to go to the comedy, but not *Shriek 3*.

You do all the right parenting things: explain why you don't want him to watch it, remind him of what usually happens when he sees scary movies, and assure him that the comedy at the Cineplex will be equally as fun, if less terrifying, and that he'll have a blast watching with his friend.

Apparently your son doesn't agree. He wheedles, begs, and sulks, but you stand firm. You're feeling great about your decision, and even your son's testiness isn't getting you down. Could there be a better parent in America at this moment?

A little later, you need to run out to the store and drop off your son on the way. You get back to your house and your spouse tells you that your son just called to ask if he could see *Shriek 3*. "I told him sure. It sounded scary—he'll love it!"

You're ready to shriek yourself. How come you're the bad cop all the time, and how do you nip your little movie mogul's manipulation in the bud?

The Solution

If there are two parents in a household, it's guaranteed their kids have figured out the best way to exploit the parent partnership to their advantage. Kids are masterful parent manipulators—they know which parent is most likely to cave in first, so they work it like there's no tomorrow. And why not? It gets them what they want.

It's key for parents, regardless whether they live together or apart and how their parenting rules may differ, to discuss and agree on certain hot topics such as movies/media, sex, drugs, and school, and present a united front to their kids. Otherwise, your kids will always be able to play one of you off the other, and in the end, nobody wins.

Here's What to Do

- Set some mutually agreed upon parameters with your partner or your children's other parent for certain situations that are relevant to your family and your children's ages; for example, what movies you will let your kids see, where they can spend the night, or how late they can stay out.

- Make a plan for addressing requests that challenge these parameters: for example, agree that if your son asks to see a movie that's questionably appropriate, you will consult with the other parent first—and let your child know that.

- When these situations arise, keep your partner in the loop: let him or her know when you've said yes or no to something and why you said it.

- If your child rushes you to make a decision and you're not ready to do so, put on the brakes—your son may want to watch *Shriek 3*, and you may eventually let him, but not right then.

Helpful Hint

A great way to discourage kids from trying to play off one parent against another is to establish a consequence for doing so. For example: your son asks you for a new video game. You say no. If he goes to ask his other parent to get a different answer, he loses his current favorite video game in addition to the opportunity of getting a new one. It's tough but fair and will work. This also works for when your children try to get out of helping around the house by telling you that their brother or sister never has to do all the chores they do.

"It's Not My Fault!"

It's early afternoon and you're enjoying the peace and quiet that can only come when all of your children are in school, when the phone rings. It's the school secretary, calling to inform you that your son won't be coming home on the bus—he'll be going to detention, instead.

Much later that afternoon, you pick up a very sullen eleven-year old from detention and get the full story. His version. According to your son, the world is full of persecution, aimed primarily at him. He was framed for a crime he didn't commit. Okay, maybe he did commit it, but it wasn't his fault. He called his friend a mean name that his teacher happened to hear, but his friend was irritating him so how could it possibly be his fault? When you point out to him that he actually did do something wrong, he looks at you, hurt, and says, "But it wasn't my fault!"

So here you are, with your child who is convinced he is a victim of gross injustice rather than a perpetrator of a petty crime. How do you help your kids learn to take responsibility for their actions?

The Solution

No defense attorney could out-argue a kid who is convinced he's been wrongly accused, and there will definitely be times when your kids may well be nabbed for things they haven't done. More often than not, though, the truth lies somewhere in between "I had nothing to do with it," and "It's all my fault." Accepting responsibility for their actions, both positive and negative, is a skill that is vital for your kids to learn.

A lot of times kids deflect the blame for things because they feel powerless over their situation—they view themselves as the victims of someone else's decision making. But regardless whether the situation involves an incident at school or misbehavior at home, by helping your kids see that they can make choices and be the boss of their own actions, you are showing them that they can take ownership for their behavior.

Here's What to Do

- Talk through the series of events with your son that led up to the incident and focus on what his role was—what he did, what decisions he made. Focus only on what your son did.

- At each step, ask your son what he could have done differently. Then ask him what might have happened if he had done it that way. This will help him see that outcomes can change based on decisions and actions.

- If your son is the only child who was puni[...]
the altercation, call the school and ask if [...]
meet with the teacher or principal.

- State in front of the principal your appr[...]
ing inappropriate behavior and that yo[...]
quences. Be sure also to ask that ever[...]
altercation suffered the same consequenc[...]
your son that you support the school's policy towa[...]
ate behavior and consequences, but let him see also that you
are his advocate by making sure that the consequences are
fairly enforced.

Helpful Hint

If your child is having a hard time being able to admit to his behavior, or make positive suggestions for what he could do differently next time, give him the chance to step back from the situation for a minute. Instead, ask him to imagine what you, his other parent, or another family member would have done in a similar circumstance and how their actions might have been different from his own. By giving your child a chance to put some distance between himself and the problem by imagining another person's reaction to it, you'll be able to help him see his own actions from a new perspective. Then you can follow up by asking him what decisions he might make next time, and compare them to the ones he's suggested for others.

I'm Sorry, Your Time Is Up

You have set a curfew for your teenage son, which, predictably, he doesn't think is late enough, and you don't think is early enough, so you're pretty sure it's probably just about right.

One night, he's out with friends and about twenty minutes before his curfew he calls to say he is going to be late. When you ask why, he tells you that he lost track of time, and he's leaving right at that moment.

You don't know what to do—on the one hand, you're proud of him for calling, since now you won't worry, but he is breaking the curfew you set—the curfew that is somewhat later than you wanted, anyway.

How do you resolve this one?

The Solution

A curfew is simply a mutually agreed upon set of rules about what your kids are allowed to do at night and when they need to be home. Being allowed to have a curfew implies that your kids are old enough and responsible enough to keep track of the time and use their time wisely. Having a curfew is a privilege, not a right.

Next time, make sure you have outlined the ground rules for emergencies, late nights, and especially changes in plan: make it an unbendable rule that if your kids want to extend their curfew, they need to call you in enough time so that if your answer is no, they can still make it home on time. If their plans change halfway through the evening, they must call and let you know how the plans have changed and where they will be. These are simple ground rules, and should be non-negotiable. If your kids can't adhere to them, then they shouldn't be allowed the privilege of having a curfew.

Here's What to Do

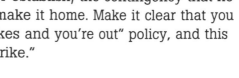

- Thank your kid for calling to say he'll be late—this shows that he is trying to be responsible and is showing respect for your rules by calling.

- Establish exactly what time he will be home that night.

- The next day reiterate (or establish) the contingency that he needs to call in time to make it home. Make it clear that you have a definite "two strikes and you're out" policy, and this incident was the first "strike."

- Let him know that if he can't manage to adhere to the above ground rule, then the privilege of going out at night unsupervised will be revoked or cut back to a much earlier time.

- Give him the opportunity to "earn" back his original curfew over time by showing that he can be responsible: running errands for you, getting to school and work on time, etc.

Helpful Hint

As much as they complain about restrictions on their lifestyle, most kids appreciate the limits that curfews set for them. Kids want to be in control of their lives, but not in total control. Parental limits give them a sense that someone else is out there as backup. Also keep in mind that as your children get older, you will need—and want—to negotiate new rules as their levels of maturity and personal responsibility grow.

For your peace of mind and their personal safety, make sure your kids have access to a cell phone or a calling card when they are out at night. That way, they'll have no excuse for not calling if plans change, and you'll know that they—and you—are just a phone call away.

Mom, I'm gonna be late.

Daughter Jekyll And Little Miss Hyde

Your daughter's middle school soccer team is participating in a big tournament in another state for the weekend. They are traveling on a bus, with parent chaperones (not you), and so you drive her to the appointed meeting place, cheer the team as they climb on the bus, and head home, proud of your daughter and hoping her team will win.

Two days later your daughter arrives home tired but happy. The tournament was great, she played well, and a good time was had by all. But not quite all, as you discover when you receive a phone call from a parent chaperone who informs you that your daughter has a repertoire of swears that would make a sailor proud, and spent much of the weekend demonstrating her cursing skills to everyone around her.

You're shocked that your daughter would behave so poorly in front of other people; she's always been a high-spirited kid, but never blatantly naughty. How do you handle this incident, and teach your daughter that her behavior away from home matters?

The Solution

Middle school is the time when formerly adorable children tend to transform into creatures from Planet Hormone—they often start to walk, talk, dress, and behave as if ill-mannered aliens have taken over their bodies. Kids this age like to take risks and push boundaries, and pushing those boundaries is much easier for them when their parents aren't around to monitor their behavior and other parents are reluctant to discipline.

With kids of every age—and especially with preteens—it's always a good idea to set your expectations for behavior beforehand, and to reiterate that your house rules apply no matter where your kids go or with whom they spend time. This will become increasingly important as your kids get older and start to go places and participate in activities that don't include you. Preteens want respect, and don't want to be treated like babies, so use that to your advantage, and make it clear that respect is a two-way street—respecting you and the rules you've set will be reciprocated with your trust. So set the ground rules, every time, for what you expect from your kids, and be clear about what the consequences will be if you are unable to trust them.

Here's What to Do

- Talk to your daughter and find out her version of the events: what are considered swears by one person may not be to another.

- Let your daughter know that regardless what happened, people were upset by her behavior—and that means that if she wants to be treated with respect by others, she'll need to act respectfully toward them, as well.

- Be clear about your expectations for her behavior the next time she's away.

- Make sure you are clear about the consequences of misbehaving.

- Let her know that you're confident she'll make appropriate decisions about behavior—reinforcing your trust in her will go a long way toward encouraging her to behave as you'd like.

Helpful Hint

No matter what age your kids are, they will inevitably be using some words that make you cringe. Whether you're dealing with bathroom talk from your four-year old or provocative posturing by your budding adolescent, teaching your kids what is and isn't acceptable in public conversation is a necessary and important job. Here are a couple of ways to help your kids be more aware of the words they choose to use:

To help young kids learn that different places are appropriate for different conversations, let them know that if they want to talk about pooping, peeing, dirty diapers, or any other apparently hysterically funny topics, they need to be in the bathroom while they are talking about them. Making this rule usually curbs excessive poop jokes, but if not, at least they are telling them in the right place.

Older kids, whose word choice can often be both colorful and annoying, usually need a strong incentive for change. So have them put their money where their mouth is: sit down with them and determine what words are taboo at your house, whether they are swears or simply unkind phrases such as, "shut up!" Then institute a fine for every time anyone, including you, says that word.

Threatening Yourself Into A Corner

You're driving a carful of kids to the pool on a hot day, and no one is very happy. The kids are driving you absolutely nuts, arguing over who touched someone else's seat, who was using someone else's air, and in general being thoroughly bratty. You start out by saying, "Kids, if you don't behave better we'll have to turn around," and hope that will do the trick. Not a chance. After fifteen more minutes of "I'm telling on you," "Did not—did too!" and a shower of thrown goldfish crackers, you lose your cool and threaten, "This is the last time I'm going to tell you to behave. If anyone does any more fighting I will turn this car around and go home instead of going to the pool!"

The car goes silent—for about a minute and a half—when one of the kids can't resist teasing another, and it all starts up again.

And now you're stuck—you don't want to spend the rest of the hot, sticky afternoon at your hot, sticky house, but you also don't want to look like a wimpy parent who doesn't follow through on her threats. So what do you do?

The Solution

It doesn't take a brain surgeon to realize that if you establish a consequence for bad behavior, you have to follow through with it. If not, there's no incentive for your kids to change their behavior. After all, yelling, "Next time and I mean it," over and over again doesn't mean anything, and both you and your kids know it. The golden rule for establishing a deterrent to misbehavior is to have an immediate and appropriate consequence.

But—if you've threatened a consequence that is going to make you miserable, too, then change it. There's no rule in the parent handbook that says you have to punish yourself while disciplining your kids, and it's easy to overreact when your kids are misbehaving—especially when it's hot and everyone is crabby. So side step without stepping back from enforcing consequences: change the consequence of the misbehavior if you think you've gone overboard or it's a punishment that outweighs the infraction. Still administer a punishment, but make it something that isn't going to be intolerable for you, too. After all, you're the boss here.

Here's What to Do

- Pull the car over to the nearest parking lot, rest area, or other safe place.

- Tell your kids that you've changed your mind about the punishment, because you don't want to punish yourself, too.

- Explain that their new punishment is to immediately clean out the car. Have bags and cleaning stuff ready.

- If your car is clean, have them pick up trash immediately around the car—cleaning up anything is a strong deterrent to misbehavior and is a community service.

- Set a time limit, and when the time is up, get them back in the car and move on with your day. If nothing else, your car and/or a small piece of the world will be a bit tidier.

Helpful Hint

To avoid making extravagant threats during the heat of the moment, set your expectations for behavior and the consequences for not meeting them before you set out on any excursion. Realistically, kids are going to argue over something when they are in the car, so make it clear how much you're going to stand and what the punishment will be. When kids know what is at stake, they often rise to the occasion.

Also, plan ahead for success: take a little time before you leave for an activity or to run errands and make sure that everyone has gone to the bathroom, has already eaten, and has brought some-thing to keep them occupied for awhile while you're in transit. This sets up some concrete expectations for behavior along the way (you aren't planning to stop at a bathroom or for snacks, for example), and by including your kids in planning ahead for something to do while you're driving, they can play an active part in making sure the trip is a success.

Easy and Effective Car Distractions

If you and your kids can't agree on which radio station to listen to, or you don't have the benefit of a book on tape to entertain them, here are some quick and easy games that kids of all ages can play:

1. *Who am I? Kids impersonate their favorite TV or movie characters with lines from their shows, while other people in the car try to guess the characters.*

2. *Geography game: One person thinks up the name of a country or place. The next person has to think of the name of a country, town, or body of water that begins with the last letter of the previous name. For example, the first person says, "Kentucky." The next person will need to think of a place that begins with "Y."*

3. *Animal guessing game: this is an animal-kingdom version of Twenty Questions. Kids take turns thinking of an animal and answering "yes" or "no" questions that others pose to them in order to guess it.*

To Catch a Thief

You and your elementary-school-aged daughter are running errands, and you stop in at a convenience store to pick up milk. While you search for a gallon of 2%, she moves off to the candy aisle to check out the latest innovations in processed sugar. You're at the checkout when your daughter brings up a candy bar and begs you to buy it for her, "Just this once because I'm so hungry and I've never had this kind and I'll never ask you for another candy bar again in my entire life."

You turn her down and tell her to put it back where she found it. She starts to argue, then sulkily stomps off back toward the candy section. On the drive home your daughter is uncharacteristically silent, and races up to her room as soon as you pull in to the driveway. You're feeling pretty lousy—it was just a candy bar, after all. Maybe you should have just let her have it. You decide to go talk to her, so you head upstairs to her room. You knock on her door and let yourself in, and discover your daughter shoving the last bit of the candy bar into her mouth. Your daughter just

stole from a store and you
drove the getaway car. The
evidence is gone—now what
do you do?

The Solution

It doesn't matter how small or inconsequential shoplifting a
candy bar may seem; you should NEVER tolerate stealing of any
kind, regardless the size of the item or the age of your child.
Whether your kids are so young they take stuff because they
don't know they shouldn't, or older and take stuff because they
want it no matter what, your kids look to you to set boundaries
and enforce the rules, and if you show them that the rules don't
apply all the time, that's the message that they'll take with them
in the future.

Although you're probably both mortified and mad, take heart: you
probably don't have a budding Bonnie or Clyde on your hands,
but rather a kid whose impulse control hasn't developed fully just
yet. So use this incident as an opportunity to reinforce your family values about honesty and theft, and teach her that stealing—
any time, any place, for any reason—is unacceptable.

Here's What to Do

- Call the store, talk to the manager, and explain both the situation that occurred and the lesson you want to teach your child.

- See if the manager is willing to participate—your purpose should be to pay for the item and have the store manager reinforce both the store's law and your family's values regarding stealing.

- Take your daughter back to the store with the candy wrapper.

- Stand with her while she explains to the cashier that she stole the candy bar and APOLOGIZES.

- Pay for the candy bar.

Helpful Hint

While most people appreciate honesty and will be lenient on young children, be aware that some stores have a mandated prosecution policy toward shoplifting, regardless the age of the offender. That means that even if the manager wants to let your child off the hook, he or she may not be allowed to. That could mean that you and your daughter are in for some legal trouble.

Where There's Smoke, There's a Liar

You have to run out to the store and your ten-year-old son doesn't want to come along. He's old enough to stay home alone for a while, so you tell him it's okay for him to be on his own. But you add your usual caveat: don't use the stove, don't answer the door, and if the phone rings, let the answering machine pick it up.

Forty-five minutes later you arrive back at home to find the windows open and a distinctly smoky smell coming from the kitchen. Your son is sitting on the couch watching TV.

When you ask what happened he looks at you innocently and says, "What? Nothing happened. Why?" You point out the open windows and the smoke and he says, "I don't know what you're talking about." You go to the kitchen and find the still-dirty pan and bring it out as evidence that he'd been cooking, and obviously not doing a very good job of it.

"I didn't do it," he insists. You're impressed with his fortitude, especially considering you know he's been the only one home, has used the stove, and left the evidence in the sink.

Your son is obviously lying, and won't admit it—what do you do next?

The Solution

You know he's lying, and he knows he's lying, so don't push it—this isn't an episode of *Law & Order*, and you both know he's definitely guilty as charged. Rather, drop the interrogation, since it's getting you nowhere, and move on to addressing the consequences of his actions. By focusing on what he did, rather than what he said, you can get to the heart of the matter— his breaking your rules—and then work on teaching him to take responsibility for his actions.

Here's What to Do

- Tell your son that you want to trust him to be responsible on his own and respect your house rules while you are gone, but you can see by his actions that you're not yet able to do so.

- Let him know that he won't be able to stay alone again until he earns back your trust—but make it clear that he can start earning back that trust immediately. If you don't give that immediate incentive, there's no motivation for him to try to earn it back at all.

- Enforce an additional, immediate consequence to reinforce the seriousness of breaking an important house—and safety—rule. This can be anything from an early bedtime that night to doing additional chores that day.

- Your son will probably fess up at this point, since most kids lie about breaking a rule because they are afraid of the consequences—and once they learn them, what's left to lie about? However, the rule you impose about leaving your son alone shouldn't change until he's had a chance to demonstrate that he's trustworthy again.

Helpful Hint

Sometimes kids break rules and step outside the boundaries because they are curious about something that's off limits to them, or they feel they are grown up enough to do more than you're letting them. So, if your son is curious about the culinary arts, or wants more responsibility around the house, take some time to cook with him—show him how to make the dish he was trying to cook on his own. Teach him how to use the stove with your supervision, and if he's truly interested in cooking, let him help you with meal preparation on a regular basis. Under your guidance, gradually let him have more responsibility for actually preparing and cooking meals, if he shows interest and enthusiasm. You'll be teaching him important skills, helping him to take on more responsibility, and giving him an opportunity to earn back your trust, at the same time—and you're getting some help in the kitchen.

Yeah, Whatever

Your daughter needs a dress for an upcoming family function, so you drive her and a small group of friends to the mall to do a little party dress shopping. Your daughter explains on the way that her friends have been chosen to accompany her based on their fashion sense; you have been chosen based on your ability to use a credit card.

So you follow your daughter and her preteen posse through the mall, stopping at various stores for a dress she will like that is also suitable for a family affair. Along the way you stop at a bookstore and agree to meet your daughter at the next store in a couple of minutes.

When you get there, your daughter's friends excitedly pull you toward the dressing room. They have found the perfect dress! You pull open the dressing room curtain, and see your daughter dressed like a 12-year-old Victoria's Secret model, complete with black bodice and filmy skirt. All she's missing are some stiletto heels and edible panties.

You say, "I'm sorry, that's not an appropriate outfit for a family party. We'll have to choose something else." She says, "Oh, yes it is! This is the dress I want!"

You say no. She says yes. You say, "I won't argue with you about this. We will look for another dress."

She turns to her friends, rolls her eyes, heaves a huge, put-out sigh, and says, "Can you believe this? I don't want another dress. That was the perfect dress for me. But yeah. Whatever. It's always about what you want and never about what I want. Thanks a lot for wrecking my life." She stalks out of the dressing room in a huge huff and you're left in her sullen wake, surrounded by a pack of petulant pre-teens.

How do you deal with backtalking behavior like that—and how can you avoid it in the future?

The Solution

Disappointment can be hard for anyone to take, especially for an adolescent, and even more so for an adolescent surrounded by her friends, all of whom are invested in the outcome of the activity. Rudeness and disrespect, however, are not acceptable, regardless the circumstances.

The most effective way to show your kids that speaking to you rudely and disrespectfully is unacceptable is to have immediate consequences for doing so. That means that if your daughter is shockingly rude to you at the mall, you're homeward bound, pronto.

One of the most important tools for negotiating through the mine-field of adolescence is to set clear and concise guidelines for everything from what you consider acceptable behavior to what is appropriate dress for your family—and make those guidelines very clear to your children before you set out to shop, visit, or socialize. If there is even a remote chance that you might be misinterpreted, rest assured you will be.

Here's What to Do

- Stop the shopping trip immediately. Tell your daughter (preferably privately, in the dressing room away from her friends, but if necessary in front of all of them) that disrespectful and rude language toward you is unacceptable, and the trip to the mall is over for that day.

- When your daughter has had time to get over her disappointment and anger (and she will be both, guaranteed), talk with her privately about your expectations for how she should talk with you.

- Set a new date for a shopping trip, but do the trip without her friends. Nothing sets up the possibility for confrontation and backtalk more than an audience of peers, if for no other reason that your kids need to save face with their friends if you assert your authority in front of them.

Helpful Hint

Whether you're going shopping for new clothes or sending your kids off to school, it's a good idea to set some guidelines for what you consider is appropriate attire for your children so your kids know in advance what is and isn't acceptable to wear. Also keep in mind that while you may not care if your daughter's thong is her most prominent wardrobe accessory, or your son's pants leave half his underwear in full view, your children's school may have other ideas. If you're stumped about how restrictive to be with your kids, check with your local school to find out its policy: most schools have a "no butts, breasts, or bellies" rule.

Their Crime, Your Punishment

You've had a family meeting and drawn up a list of basic house rules, like, "use words that show respect for each other," and "put away what you get out"—you know, the usual basic rules of decent family dynamics that you'd assume most families should have but that you wrote down, just in case. And a good thing, too, since your daughter broke every single one of them during an especially crabby afternoon.

So you and your daughter sat down and discussed what the consequences of breaking all of the house rules should be, and she decided that a good consequence for this instance would be not to be allowed to sleep over at anyone's house for the next two days. You're pretty sure she chose this because no one had invited her over, but you're proud of her for coming up with a solution on her own, and agree.

That very evening your daughter gets the call: she's invited to a sleepover the next night at her very best friend's house. Predictably, your daughter wants to rescind her punishment and is determined to convince you, too, no matter what it takes. She bargains, pleads, argues, and finally has a full-blown tantrum about the issue. Her punishment has suddenly become your punishment, too, and you're not sure what to do. You want to stick to your principles—and after all, this was her idea—but this is ridiculous. What do you do now?

The Solution

Teaching your kids to accept the consequences of their actions is a hard but necessary lesson, and part of being a parent is taking on the role of the very unpopular Rule Enforcer. Sure, it's hard for kids when they miss out on something fun because they get in trouble, but it's called "punishment" for a reason.

It's great to include kids in the discipline process; after all, one of the meanings of "discipline" is "to learn." But make sure that when you sit down together to decide what the consequences of breaking rules should be, your kids understand the specific details, such as when it starts, when it ends, and what it entails. Consider putting it in writing and posting in the refrigerator so everyone can see—and remember—what you agreed to.

You may find that when you let your kids help decide what their punishment should be, it's much harsher than anything you'd come up with yourself. Help your kids tone down those, "I shouldn't be allowed to play outside for the rest of the summer" kinds of consequences to more reasonable ones.

Then if your kids moan and groan about the punishment or want to change it because it interferes with something they want to do, stick to your guns. Make it clear that if they are mature enough to be allowed to help decide their punishment, they are mature enough to accept it.

Here's What to Do

- Decide together what the punishment should entail.

- Be specific about details: when it starts, when it ends, how long it lasts, and what specific privileges are revoked.

- Post the details in a place where everyone can see—and remember—what they are.

- Enforce the punishment calmly but firmly: remember, you're your children's parent, not their friend. You're showing your kids that you stick to your word, and this will matter to them in the future.

- When the punishment is over, let it go and move on.

Helpful Hint

Wondering what your house rules should be? Start with the basics, and post them where everyone—not just the kids—can see them every day. Just having them in constant view will remind all of your family members that you have rules. Here is a list of some standard house rules:

- *Adults are the boss—don't argue with their decisions.*
- *Use words of respect: no swearing, no bathroom talk.*
- *Do what you're asked with no whining.*
- *Pick up and put away what you get out.*
- *Remember we are a team!*

Appendix
Ideas and Suggestions
for Family Serenity

While kid-centric squabbles are as inevitable as pink eye, the best way to handle family conflicts is to try to avoid them altogether. This section is a grab bag of suggestions and ideas for how to circumvent potential problems before they start and for maintaining your family's serenity—and your sanity. You'll find suggestions ranging from how to set up a chore system to how to back away from confrontations with your kids without backing down. Also included are ideas for how to establish a set of rules for your family, and games and activities to help improve family communication.

Remember that no matter how hard you try to be a perfect parent, and how much you love your kids, you're probably going to yell at them from time to time and feel lousy about it. They are probably going to fight, tattle, occasionally do naughty things and lie about them, and will ask you to pay them for jobs you do every day of the week for free. That's how being a family works, and no family is perfect. So relax—you're doing fine.

Chores

As much as your kids may grumble about helping around the house, you are actually doing them a favor by assigning them chores. Studies have shown even simple, regular household responsibilities can enhance a child's self esteem and self confidence, and help them connect more closely with their families. So if you thought assigning your kids jobs around the house only meant that you were getting a little help with the vacuuming, think again.

So how do you get your kids happily enhancing their self esteem, and self confidence, and connecting to your family?

Keep their chores, and your expectations, age-appropriate:
A ten-year old will obviously be capable of completing most chores better than his four-year-old little brother, and generally will be able to accomplish more complicated jobs. But don't expect a professional job from any of your children. Rather, keep your expectations for what they can do and the quality of their work realistic—and remember that "good enough" is usually "good enough." If you want a professionally cleaned house, hire a professional.

Show your kids what you want: Most kids learn best by watching—and practicing—through hands-on learning. You can't expect your kids to know how to rake the yard properly if they've never done it before. So show them what you expect: go step-by-step through the jobs you want your kids to do, first showing them how, then doing it with them, then finally letting them do it on their own with your supervision. Eventually they will be able to do most jobs without constant supervision.

It's usually a good idea to write down the specific steps for jobs you want them to complete and post them somewhere for your kids to see and refer to every time, or use photographs of what a completed job should look like so they have a frame of reference.

Let your kids know they've done a good job: Sure, their beds are a little lumpy, or they missed a few patches of grass, but they did the best job they could. So tell them—let your children know that you're proud of their efforts, and that you've noticed their work and contribution to the family. Remember that a little positive reinforcement goes a long way, whether it's in the form of a treat or some enthusiastic praise.

Keep them responsible for their contributions to the family: It's easy to let chores slip when you and your kids are busy with school, sports, or other activities, but giving up and doing them yourself because it's faster, or letting your kids slide by regularly doesn't help anyone. It's a good idea to have either a formal or informal contract with your kids that states that special activities and extracurricular fun is contingent on accomplishing their daily or weekly chores. Many families write up a chore contract and post it as a visible reminder of what needs to be done around the house before other, more fun stuff, happens.

Remember that it's a lot of work: You'd think that assigning your kids chores would mean less work for you, but be aware that you'll still spend a lot of time and effort motivating and monitoring your kids' progress. By sticking with it you'll not only show your kids that being part of a family means everybody contributes to the family's upkeep, but also you're showing your kids good parenting in action.

Suggestions For Family Chores

Here are some suggestions for common household chores that kids of a variety of ages are capable of accomplishing. Please note that these recommendations are based on very general developmental milestones, so are merely guidelines for children—your child might be much more developmentally advanced and therefore capable of more than indicated.

Children ages 3 to 5 years

(Please note that any job assigned to a three-year old will need to be carefully supervised)

- Put napkins or spoons on the table
- Carry plastic condiments from the refrigerator to the table
- Help sort laundry by colors
- Sort toys by color or function
- Pick up toys and place them in a toybox or basket with direction
- Help sort child-safe silverware by function: fork, knife, spoon
- Help put pillows or stuffed animals, etc. on bed
- Put away own pajamas
- Help water household plants
- Place dirty laundry in hamper

Children ages 6 to 8 years

All of the above plus:

- Put silverware on table (note that most six-year olds will need help setting the table accurately)
- Clear the table of unbreakable items
- Feed pets
- Put away toys and tidy room with direction
- Make bed with help
- Help clean trash and toys from car with direction/supervision

Children ages 8 to 10 years

All of the above plus:

- Set table
- Clear table
- Sweep floor
- Use vacuum cleaner
- Clean room (with direction)
- Stack wood with assistance
- Take out trash
- Wash windows
- Unload dishwasher

Children 10 and up

All of the above plus:

- Shovel snow
- Rake leaves
- Water lawn
- Plant and weed garden beds
- Use a lawnmower with careful supervision
- Use non-toxic cleaning agents with supervision
- Use iron with supervision

Suggestions For Family Rules

Wondering how to rally your family into a cohesive, happy unit, ready to take on the world as a team? Making a set of family rules can go a long way toward creating positive family dynamics. Here are some steps you can take to create a list of rules that works for your family:

1. Sit down with your kids and discuss what you think are the most important issues your family faces. (For example, being respectful of other family members, keeping the house tidy, being honest, and so on.)

2. Create a short list of rules you all agree to follow, and make sure everyone in the family understands the reasons for them. The list needs to be short enough so that everyone in the family can follow all of them—a rules list that contains twenty different guidelines for family behavior, for example, is one that no one can adhere to.

3. Keep the rules specific enough so that everyone can follow them and succeed. For example, if a family priority is to have a tidy house, the rule shouldn't be, "Clean the house," but could instead be, "Pick up the toys you play with."

4. Establish clear consequences for breaking the rules. Your kids will be more likely to follow rules if they know there are risks involved in breaking them.

5. Write down the rules and consequences for breaking them and post them where everyone—kids and adults—can see them and refer to them every day.

6. Enforce the rules consistently. It's confusing for kids to have rules mean something one day, and not the next.

Feeling stumped?

Here are some suggestions for general family rules that work well and are time-tested:

- Use words of respect
- Put back what you play with or use (or cook with, clean with, and so on)
- Turn off the lights when you leave a room
- Acknowledge it when someone does something nice for you
- Be forgiving
- Apologize when you should
- Tell the truth
- Be a team player

Helpful Hint

Whether they'll admit it or not, kids love rules. They thrive on the sense of order rules make in their lives, and while they also like to see just how far they can push against the boundaries adults set for them, those same boundaries make them feel safe.

Ideas For Avoiding Showdowns: Knowing When to Say When

Seemingly minor squabbles with your kids can quickly escalate into big power struggles if your kids feel they have no control over the situation. You can help avoid these blow ups by learning to step back and disengage from the confrontation. Stepping back doesn't mean backing down—you don't have to acquiesce to your sulking teenager's whims, or let your toddler walk all over you. Rather, it involves maintaining your cool, offering choices, and providing your kids with a way out of the potentially volatile situation—something they usually can't do on their own. Here are ways to avoid head-to-head confrontations with your kids, depending on their ages.

For younger kids (3 to 8-year olds):

Transition times, such as getting ready for bed, school, or meals, are usually hardest for young children to handle, since it means breaking away from one activity to pursue another—usually not on their preferred schedule. If you're in a situation that could lead to confrontation, make sure you don't ask rhetorical, open-ended questions that could spark a power struggle. For example, saying to your five-year old, "Are you ready to go to bed?" is begging for a fight. Rather, give your children a choice between two very specific options related to what you want them to do: "Would you like to put on your pajamas or brush your teeth first tonight?" A question like this makes it understood that it's bedtime, that your child is going, and that you are in charge of the situation—but the fact that he can make choices also offers him a measure of personal control.

For older kids (8 years and up):

Older kids will push the boundaries as hard as they can, and the more you react, the less in control they'll feel, and so the harder they push back. You can avoid this vicious, "Who's the boss here?" cycle simply by disengaging from it altogether. Stay calm. Let your kids know that you are aware of how they are feeling, but that you aren't going to participate. For example, if your daughter is disappointed because she isn't allowed to go to the movies on a school night and is trying to pick a fight about it with you, you could say, "I know you're upset about not being allowed to go to the movies and want to argue with me about it, but I'm not going to do it." And then stick to your word—don't get sucked back in until tempers have cooled. When your daughter has calmed down, talk with her about why she was so upset, and ask her to come up with ways she can better express those feelings.

Games And Activities to Promote Family Harmony

If you're struggling for ways to improve your family dynamics, or just want to have some good old-fashioned family fun together, try some of these games and activities that promote positive family communication. You might be surprised what you learn about each other.

Charades

This game is an oldie but a goodie, and it promotes healthy and positive family interactions. Kids of all ages can play charades. It is a game that lets everyone in a family be seen, heard, and watched by other family members, and lets each family member be the center of attention in a positive, fun way.

Participants are divided into two teams. Each team thinks of titles of movies, books, or television shows that are familiar to all family members, and writes them on slips of paper, which should then be collected and placed in a hat or bowl. Players from each team take turns drawing the names from the hat and silently acting out the name while being timed. The team that takes the least amount of time guessing correctly wins.

The Name Game

This is a game similar to charades, but doesn't require any acting. Participants are divided into two teams. Each team writes down the names of people your family knows well: they can be actors, sports figures, cartoon characters, neighbors, famous people—anyone who will be recognized by your family members. All the names are put into a hat. Players from each team take turns drawing names from the hat. The player who draws the name describes the person or character whose name they've drawn without naming him or her while his/her team guesses who it is. Each team gets one minute per round to guess as many names as possible. Whichever teams guesses the most names in five rounds wins.

"That's the Way I See It"

The goal of this game is to let your kids show you how they view your family, and how they'd like to view your family. Each child will have a turn being director. The director tells each family member what to do, based on how he or she sees that person's role in the family. For example, the director might tell one parent to stand in a corner away from everyone else, working on a project that no one can interrupt, if that's the way that child sees that parent's role in the family, or tell another to rush around the room in a frenzy, or sit quietly with a child on his or her lap. Let each child in your family be the director, assigning the other family members the roles he or she sees them playing. After all the kids have a turn, spend some time talking about how they feel about the way your family currently interacts, and how

they'd like your family to interact.
Then let your kids assign the roles
that would create the family they'd
like to see.

Take a Walk in Your Family's Shoes

A good way to teach younger children about respecting and
being tolerant of other people is to encourage them to "take a
walk in someone else's shoes." Have them mentally switch
places with someone else in the family and ask them questions
based on their character's behavior. How would they feel being
the oldest child and having more responsibility? Would they
want a little brother or sister taking things from their room without asking? What would it be like to be the youngest child, or the
only girl, or an only child? What would they want other people
in the family to notice about them? This is a game that kids play
remarkably well, and you may be surprised at the sophisticated
and thoughtful responses they give when they are walking in
someone else's shoes.

About the Authors

Lauri Berkenkamp

Lauri Berkenkamp lives with her husband and four children in Vermont. Lauri holds a master's degree in English Literature from the University of Vermont and is a former faculty member of Vermont College of Norwich University in Montpelier, Vermont. She is the author of *"Mom, the Toilet's Clogged!" Kid Disasters and How to Fix Them*, and the co-author of *Teaching Your Children Good Manners* and *Talking to Your Kids About Sex: From Toddlers to Preteens* as well as several other books.

Steven C. Atkins, Psy.D.

Steven C. Atkins, Psy.D. is a licensed psychologist, instructor, and clinical associate at Dartmouth Medical School's Department of Child Psychiatry, specializing in specific learning disabilities, ADHD, and developmental theory. He holds a master's degree in Education from Harvard University and a doctorate in Psychology from the Massachusetts School of Professional Psychology. He is the co-author of *Teaching Your Children Good Manners* and *Talking to Your Kids About Sex: From Toddlers to Preteens*. Dr. Atkins lives in the Upper Valley of New Hampshire.

Here's What's Being Said About
Go Parents! guides™

Praise for *"Mom, The Toilet's Clogged!"*
Kid Disasters and How to Fix Them:

"Whether your child licks a frozen flagpole or plays pattycake with a cactus, this book has the solution. *"Mom, the Toilet's Clogged!" Kid Disasters and How to Fix Them* is a great gift for any parent, grandparent or person with a retainer stuck in the garbage disposer."

—**Tim Bete**
Award-winning humor columnist and father of three

". . . *Kid Disasters and How to Fix Them* is a handy-dandy compendium for anyone, especially those with kids in residence. Author Lauri Berkenkamp offers no-nonsense solutions to a myriad of child-related catastrophes. Her directions are clear and her remedies call for items found at home such as peanut butter, scissors and white glue. Readers with fly-paper minds will delight in the off-beat facts sprinkled throughout the book. Zippy illustrations combined with Berkenkamp's solid, chatty advice makes this book a winner."

—**Nancy Nash-Cummings**
Nationally syndicated columnist ("Ask Ann and Nan")
and co-author of *Clean It, Find It, Fix It*

Praise for *Teaching Your Children Good Manners*:

"Filled with sensible advice, *Teaching Your Children Good Manners* gives frazzled parents the practical tools they need to teach their kids—whatever their ages—to treat others with respect, kindness, and consideration. And really, what's more important than that?"

—Armin Brott
Author of *The Expectant Father: Facts, Tips, and Advice for Dads-to-Be* and *A Dad's Guide to the Toddler Years*

"Wow! *Teaching Your Children Good Manners* is the best survival book for parents I have read. Everyone talks about social skills, finally a creative, practical, fun, developmentally appropriate book focuses on teaching skills every child needs. *Teaching Your Children Good Manners* is a must read for parents of children of all ages. Follow these suggestions and your friends will be amazed at your children's maturity. And, you will be amazed at how their new skills help them succeed."

—Dr. Ken West
Author of *The Shelbys Need Help!*
A Choose-Your-Own Solution and Adventure Book

"A genuinely entertaining guide that gives parents important guidelines to calm their nerves when it comes to teaching their children good manners now, and for life."

—Myrna B. Shure, Ph.D.
Author of *Raising A Thinking Preteen*

Teaching Your Children Good Manners is a 2002 Parents Choice Approved award winner!

Praise for *Talking to Your Kids About Sex: From Toddlers to Preteens*:

"At last, a guide for beleagured parents who want to talk to their children about 'the facts of life' but are uncertain even about how to begin. This accessible and entertaining book provides just the right blend of advice, activities and answers for an often-daunting task. Filled with warmth and humor, it is respectful to the range of parenting styles and to the developmental needs of children. In this sex-saturated culture, where peers and media provide so much of the (mis)information kids get, help for parents is here!"

—**Martha B. Straus, Ph.D.** Clinical psychologist and author of *No-Talk Therapy for Children and Adolescents*

"I was delighted to read Lauri Berkenkamp and Steven Atkins' new book, *Talking to Your Kids About Sex*, which is truly the best I have read on the subject. *Talking To Your Kids About Sex* provides parents with all of the information they need about what to expect from their children, developmental reference points, frequently asked questions, and exceptional suggestions about the ways in which parents can help their children learn to appreciate, respect, and protect their bodies. Berkenkamp and Atkins present examples and points of information that are masterfully designed to diminish a parent's anxiety in dealing with the questions and issues pertaining to the topic of sexuality. They accomplish this in witty, humorous, and quietly brilliant style."

—Dr. Mary Lamia, host of **KidTalk with Dr. Mary** as heard on Radio Disney AM 1310 KMKY and AM 1470 KIID